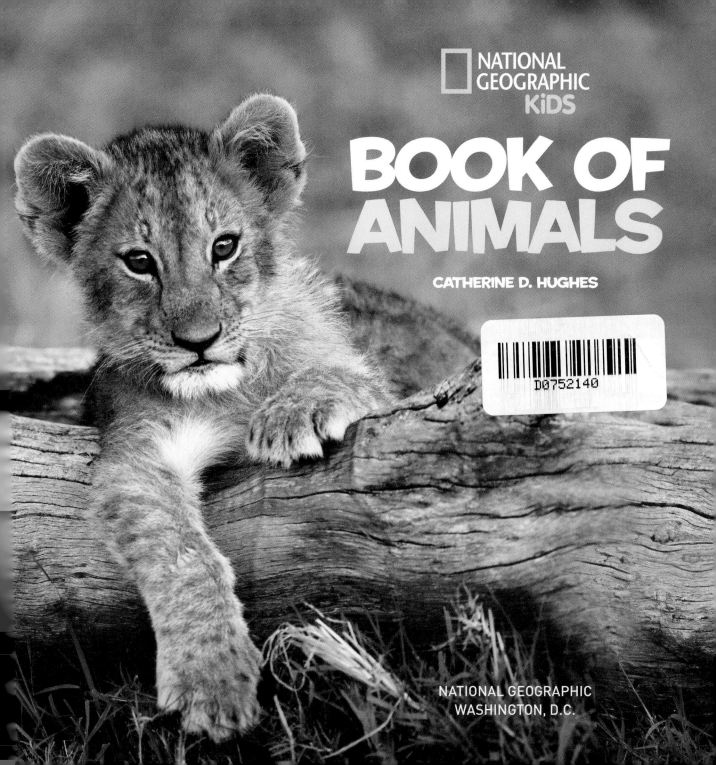

NATIONAL
GEOGRAPHIC
KiDS

BOOK OF ANIMALS

CATHERINE D. HUGHES

NATIONAL GEOGRAPHIC
WASHINGTON, D.C.

Lions often **HUNT TOGETHER** in a group.

FACTS

KIND OF ANIMAL
mammal

HOME
parts of Africa and a
small area in India

SIZE
weighs about as much
as one or two men

FOOD
gazelles, zebras, hares,
and other animals

SOUNDS
roar, purr, snarl, hiss

BABIES
three to five at a time

LION

Lions live in prides.

Lions are the only wild cats that live in family groups called prides. Lion cubs have many playmates in their pride.

A playful lion cub finds toys easily. Even a stick becomes a toy.

BLACK-HANDED SPIDER MONKEY

Monkeys are at home in the trees.

Black-handed spider monkeys are acrobats. They swing from branch to branch. Sometimes they leap to the next tree.

Black-handed spider monkeys rarely come out of the treetops.

When a baby black-handed spider monkey is **ONE YEAR OLD** it can climb by itself.

Male humpback **WHALES SING.** A whale's song can last 15 minutes.

Whales come to the surface of the ocean to **BREATHE.** Humpback whales can hold their breath for up to **30 MINUTES.**

FACTS

KIND OF ANIMAL
mammal

HOME
oceans worldwide

SIZE
about as long as a big bus

FOOD
shrimplike krill, small fish

SOUNDS
squeal, grunt, moan, and sounds too low for humans to hear

BABIES
one at a time

HUMPBACK WHALE

Humpbacks do not have teeth.

There are many kinds of whales. Some have teeth. Others do not.

The humpback whale has baleen instead of teeth. Baleen hangs from the whale's upper jaw.

UPPER JAW

BALEEN

ARIZONA
CORAL SNAKE
Bright colors send a message.

A coral snake's bright colors warn, "I'm poisonous, so stay away!" The colors remind predators, or enemies that might attack, to leave this kind of snake alone.

Arizona coral snakes are small, and their teeth are very short. They use their poison mainly to kill small animals to eat, such as lizards and other snakes.

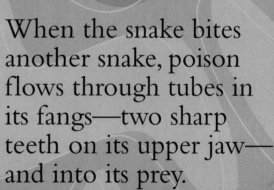

Arizona coral snakes are **SHY.** They spend a lot of time under rocks or dirt and usually **HUNT AT NIGHT.**

When the snake bites another snake, poison flows through tubes in its fangs—two sharp teeth on its upper jaw— and into its prey.

Have you ever seen a snake?

ZEBRA
Stripes confuse enemies.

A zebra looks like a horse with stripes. Every zebra's stripes are a little bit different.

Zebras **SLEEP STANDING** up.

Zebras live in family groups called herds. It is important for a zebra family to stay together for protection.

There are **THREE SPECIES,** or kinds, of zebras.

Zebras' stripes confuse animals that hunt them. The jumble of stripes makes it hard to see where one zebra ends and another begins.

A baby zebra is called a foal. It can walk when it is only 20 minutes old. An hour after it is born, the foal can run.

FACTS

KIND OF ANIMAL
mammal

HOME
parts of Africa

SIZE
about as tall as a small horse

FOOD
mostly grass, some leaves and twigs

SOUNDS
bray, bark, soft snort

BABIES
one at a time

How old were you when you learned to walk?

HARP SEAL

This seal's coat changes color.

A mother harp seal takes good care of her baby. The baby is called a pup. At first, the pup doesn't look like Mom.

A harp seal can **HOLD ITS BREATH** underwater for 20 minutes. Then it comes to the surface to breathe.

A pup's fluffy white fur helps keep it warm on the ice, where it is born.

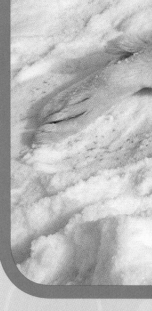

A harp seal pup may gain about **80 POUNDS** in 12 days by drinking its **MOTHER'S MILK.**

FACTS

KIND OF ANIMAL
mammal

HOME
North Atlantic and Arctic Oceans

SIZE
weighs about as much as a big professional football player

FOOD
mostly fish

SOUNDS
grunt, bleat

BABIES
one at a time

SEA OTTER

Thick fur keeps otters warm.

FACTS

KIND OF ANIMAL
mammal

HOME
coastal areas of northern and eastern North Pacific Ocean

SIZE
weighs about as much as two four-year-olds

FOOD
sea animals such as sea urchins, crabs, snails, clams, abalone

SOUNDS
coo, whine, whistle, growl

BABIES
usually one at a time

Sea otters are expert swimmers. Their thick, fluffy fur keeps them warm in cold ocean water.

Sea otters make sure their fur is very clean so that it will keep them warm. Otters spend hours every day cleaning themselves.

When a sea otter **DIVES,** its **EARS AND NOSE** close tightly to keep water out.

FACTS

KIND OF ANIMAL
mammal

HOME
parts of Africa

SIZE
about as tall as three men standing on each other's shoulders

FOOD
leaves

SOUNDS
hiss, bellow, whistle, grunt, snort, bleat

BABIES
usually one at a time; sometimes two

GIRAFFE

Giraffes are the tallest land animals.

A giraffe's legs are taller than most grown-up people. Its long neck adds even more to its height.

A giraffe **PROTECTS ITSELF** from enemies by **KICKING.**

Giraffes eat leaves. Because they are so tall, giraffes can reach leaves growing high in trees.

BLACK-AND-YELLOW GARDEN SPIDER

A garden spider builds a web.

The garden spider builds a web to trap insects to eat. The web is made of spider silk. Spider silk is a sticky thread that is made inside the spider's body.

BABY SPIDERS are called spiderlings.

FEMALE, or girl, black-and-yellow garden spiders build **BIGGER WEBS** than male, or boy, spiders.

The spider attaches silk threads to grasses or other plants. Then it stretches more silk, making a pattern in a circle.

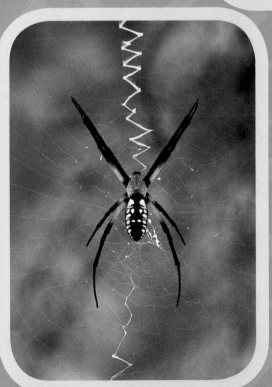

The spider weaves a zigzag line in the web. That is where the spider usually waits for an insect to fly into the web and get stuck. That insect becomes the spider's supper.

FACTS

KIND OF ANIMAL
arachnid

HOME
much of North America

SIZE
about as big as the spider in the photo at left

FOOD
flies, beetles, wasps, grasshoppers, and other flying insects

SOUNDS
none

BABIES
up to 1,400 eggs at a time

Can you draw a spiderweb?

CAMEL

Camels have humps.

FACTS

KIND OF ANIMAL
mammal

HOME
Bactrian: dry areas of Mongolia and China; Dromedary: dry areas of North Africa and the Middle East

SIZE
a little taller than a very tall man

FOOD
many different kinds of plants

SOUNDS
moan, groan, bleat, bellow, roar, rumble

BABIES
usually one at a time

You probably know that camels have humps.
Did you know that there are two species of camels?
One has two humps. The other has one hump.

Bactrian camels have two humps.
Dromedary camels have one hump.

MOUNTAIN GORILLA

Gorillas live in groups called troops.

A troop may have 30 gorillas. The biggest male is the leader of the family group. Called a silverback, he has silver fur on his back.

There are often other male gorillas in the troop. Females and babies make up the rest of the family.

FACTS

KIND OF ANIMAL
mammal

HOME
two areas in central Africa

SIZE
male: about as tall as a tall man; female: about as tall as a short woman

FOOD
leaves, roots, shoots, fruits, wild celery, tree bark and pulp; sometimes insects

SOUNDS
roar, grunt, bark, and hoot

BABIES
one at a time

PARENT TIPS

Extend your child's experience beyond the pages of this book. A visit to the zoo is one great way to continue satisfying your child's curiosity about wildlife. Make a list of the animals in this book and take it with you. At the zoo, have your child check off the animals you see. Here are some other activities you can do with the *National Geographic Kids Book of Animals*.

GET DRESSED
(INDEPENDENCE)
Zebras have black-and-white-stripes (p. 10). Have a family zebra day when all of you dress in black-and-white clothing or you all wear stripes.

MEASURE HEIGHT
(MATH)
Giraffes are tall (p. 16). Use a tape measure to determine how high up a wall your child can reach with her hand while standing flat-footed. Compare that height with the height she can reach on her tiptoes.

TAKE A WALK
(EXPLORING)
Garden spiders build webs (p. 18). Go on a spiderweb hunt. Early morning is a great time to spot webs in gardens and meadows because dew helps make webs more visible. Take along a picnic!

TREASURE HUNT
(COOPERATION)
Lions live in prides (p. 2). Have two or three of your child's friends over for playtime. Read them the gray wolf and lion pages in the book. Suggest that they cooperate to achieve a goal, just as wolves and lions do.

The goal could be figuring out clues to a simple treasure hunt. Give the children a clue to find the next clue. By successfully solving all the clues—using teamwork—they find the "prize." Provide a prize for each of them, or make the prize something that continues cooperation and sharing (for example, cookies to share, a trip together to a playground, art supplies they can all use, or a game they can play together).

WEATHER CHECK
(MEASURING TEMPERATURE)
Sea otters have thick fur to stay warm (p. 14). Using a weather thermometer, help your child measure the temperature of the inside of your house and compare it to the outside (if different), and to the temperature inside the freezer or refrigerator. Talk about hot and cold temperatures inside versus outside, winter versus summer, etc.

SILLY TALK
(HUMOR)
Humpback whales have no teeth (p. 6). Curl your lips over your teeth to show your child how to play a game of "guess what I said" as you each take turns talking "with no teeth."

COLOR SYMBOLS
(OBSERVATION)
Coral snakes' bright colors send a message (p. 8). Talk with your child about bright colors that send messages in your everyday life. Guide him with examples: a red traffic light or stop sign mean stop; green traffic light means go; and yellow is the color for caution. Ask your child what different colors make him think of or how different colors make him feel.

FROZEN JUICE
(FOLLOWING RECIPE)
Camels' bodies help them stay cool in the hot desert (p. 20). On a hot day, make "juicicles" with your child to help cool off. Freeze juice in ice-cube trays. Insert Popsicle sticks to hold the treats.

CLIMB A TREE
(COORDINATION)
Spider monkeys are at home in the trees (p. 4). If you see an appropriately sturdy tree with low branches, help your child climb and play in it. He can hang from a branch and pretend to be a monkey.

FOLLOW THE LEADER
(EXERCISE)
Gorillas live in troops and are led by an adult male (p. 22). Play follow the leader as a family. Take turns being the leader.

RHYME WORDS
(LANGUAGE)
Harp seals change their coats (p. 12). Encourage your child to make up a poem or a series of rhyming sentences about seals. Start your child off by asking him what rhymes with "seal" (meal, feel, steal, real, peel, etc.) Then suggest that he make up two funny sentences that rhyme. (Give an example, e.g., "My harp seal made me a *meal*." or "Where did you put the *peel*, you silly *seal*?")